LET THE CHILDREN WRITE

TO BERNARD

My stimulus now and
always

Let the Children Write

An Explanation of Intensive Writing by
MARGARET LANGDON B.A. N.F.F.
Introduction by Miss G. C. Whitwill M.A.
Illustrated by the author

LONGMANS

LONGMANS, GREEN AND CO LTD
London and Harlow
*Associated companies, branches and representatives
throughout the world*

© MARGARET LANGDON 1961
FIRST PUBLISHED 1961
SEVENTH IMPRESSION 1969

PRINTED IN GREAT BRITAIN BY
LOWE AND BRYDONE (PRINTERS) LTD., LONDON

Introduction

WHEN I RECEIVED from Mrs. Langdon a copy of *Intensive Writing* with its selection of her children's work, I acclaimed with delight and some excitement this further proof of the fulfilment of the promise shown when, as an inexperienced graduate, she took her first school practice. Over the years I have seen with mounting pleasure her inspiring work with children in primary schools and now has come this delightful experiment in written English with children of the secondary school age. Here, indeed, is a result of a clear conception of what education should mean and of a rare understanding of children.

The response of teachers from many countries to *Intensive Writing* has prompted Mrs. Langdon to give us this book, *Let the Children Write*. It is a vivid, succinct and often moving account of her experiment and, further, it is creative. Mrs. Langdon has thought out her problem anew from the point of view of the children's needs and of what they are responsive to in literature at their stage of development. It is in this analysis of her problem and its application in the classroom that she has found a way to set the children free to do their own creative work.

Much has been given us on the teaching of written English in schools but in general this is concerned with preparing for the child's writing in the future. Mrs. Langdon's starting point is the child as he is now with the needs, interests and abilities of his stage of development.

With this new starting point comes a new emphasis on the need for expression, but the expression of a lived experience with the emotions, the imagery, and the words that are the child's. The children's 'poems', vivid, genuine, with so much beauty and withal so revealing, are their response to this encouragement to express. The experiment, starting as an exploration, has certainly led to discovery. Scope for the expression of emotion in a form that demands effort and brings satisfaction may well be the heart of the matter and have relevance to wider educational problems that all teachers face.

I personally await with eagerness further exploration by Mrs. Langdon with children both younger and older than those of the initial group.

In the meantime, may this book go out to inspire and to encourage teachers to *Let the Children Write* what they need to, want to, and can write, here and now.

G. C. WHITWILL

Contents

[*1*]

An Experiment in Expression

IT ALL STARTED with boredom—boredom and disappointment. I expect you would be bored by the time you had reached the end of the thirtieth essay. Immature thoughts, immature expressions, immature writing—oh dear! I always start on a pile of exercise books with high hopes that here, in this set, will be the essay which will justify my teaching, the essay with a flash of genius in the turn of a phrase, in the breath of an idea. I mark one, then another, and yet another, scratching through the dumb phrases, the uninspired thoughts, the platitudinous expressions, and end with an unenthusiastic 'Fair', and a private thought, 'What's the use?'

That thought became gradually more and more of an obsession with me. True, I was teaching in a village school, an all-range school at that. The children were a mixture, rising from educationally subnormal, with a medical certificate to prove it, to just failed scholarship, with a psychological hangover to prove that. They were promoted as they came of age, with the result that a class of thirty really was thirty, at thirty different stages, demanding thirty different lessons at the same time.

To add to the hopelessness of the situation, my classroom was part of the original hundred-year-old school. True, we had had, lately, additions and renovations, but the room in which my children sat, dreamed and worked, was, to say the least of it, uninspiring. Small and dingy, it had that indescribable school smell of books, bodies, perspiration, plimsolls, dust, chalk and age. (Air-spray kills it momentarily, I've found, and the children love to press the trigger.)

In this surrounding, with its daily grind against low standards and poor conditions, my despondency grew. I felt a poor teacher. I felt that my own flame of creation had burnt so low that I couldn't kindle anything in the children, and could only offer them a dull, dutiful, do-it-because-you-must kind of lesson.

The only reason why I didn't resign there and then was the friendliness of the children. Away from the dry-as-dust atmosphere of the class-room, the children would chat freely of their adventures, thoughts, ideas, dreams and fears. I would listen with interest as their young, excited voices clamoured to be heard. Here was no stiffness of expression, dullness of phrase, no stilted, lifeless thought. Here, pouring out, was the very stuff of life, pulsating and vibrating with vigour and individuality. They were eager to express, to tell, to put into words.

Perhaps it was the writing? So I scrambled into a babble of oral lessons. Lecturettes (dreadful word!), talks, debates, discussions. No! No! No! Still there was none of that delightful, spontaneous individuality. Here, as in their written work, I felt that the children were using a medium which was unnatural to them—a stultifying, deadening medium, which made all their expression come out as from a sausage machine, in a string of dull, stodgy sausages of things which they thought they *ought* to write, and say and think.

It was harder for me to bear the dullness of expression, because I have always been aware of the value of words. They excite me. At the same time, the relationship between truth and expression is very real to me, and I am uncomfortable when people try to cloak a hypocritical thought with a platitudinous phrase. I feel very strongly that people should think for themselves, and say what they think.

How was I to get this over to the children? Obviously they were being embarrassed by the conventional methods of expression which is expected from them at school. I knew they had the thoughts, the ideas, the experiences: how could I help them to express these in an acceptable educational form, without brushing the dust from the butterflies' wings as I did so?

Wordsworth talks of 'emotion recollected in tranquillity', and it was from the idea of feeling that I started my search for a new expressive medium. Poetry is the natural medium of emotion in writing, but I knew at once that this was a dead end as far as modern children are concerned. In these days, if anything is more soul destroying than marking essays, it is teaching poetry to teenagers. Do you recognize (and I'm sure you do if you have had anything to do with children of twelve to sixteen years of age) that blank, withdrawn, politely supercilious look which curtains their faces when they feel that you are being particularly 'square'? Any normal poetry lesson produces that look; so, firmly, my medium must be non-poetic.

Emotional, non-poetic, I was getting on a bit. What else?

Brevity, I felt, was an essential. Much as children loved to babble on in their talk, when it came to writing, any inspiration which they had, took wings when confronted by the stern 'Two pages at least' or 'Not less than 250 words'. Have you seen children stop and count and add a bit more, and count again? And they are supposed to be creating! For normal essays, when asked, 'How much have we to write?' I firmly insisted, 'Start at the beginning and go on until you have reached the end'. I felt that length should be no criterion of value.

Because of brevity, simplicity became an essential. All the padding, the filling in, the stretching out, of one poor small idea, could be left out, and the idea, stated clearly and briefly, could stand on its own merits—could even grow in stature because it had to be thought out clearly, in order to be expressed simply. One idea, or experience told simply in two words or two lines is surely better than two pages filled with meaningless words, written in order to fill the space. I thought of the dignity and simplicity of Biblical language and decided that I was on the right track.

All that I had to do now, was to perform the Herculean task of encouraging the children to re-collect an emotional experience and express it briefly, simply and with honesty. It was the emotion part which gave me most trouble. How was I to get an emotion over, naturally, easily and without causing them to be embarrassed?

As these children were due to take an external examination in English, I felt I must continue their conventional lessons as normally as possible, but that I could spare one half-hour period a week to attempt a new, drastic experiment.

April 1st gave me my first real break.

The Spider on the Wall

IT HAPPENED THAT April 1st was a weekday. For several years we have either been on holiday with an early Easter or, luckily, it has fallen on a Saturday. This year it fell on a school day and I could tell from the glint in the teenagers' eyes that they had not overlooked the fact. But they are only children after all, and shoe-laces, mysterious packages, empty egg-shells and imaginary spiders brought back my own childhood efforts. I could still remember vividly the horror with which I had tried to brush off that—Spider! Imaginary Spider! Here was my opportunity to produce a strong emotion, yet a completely unembarrassing one.

The class was waiting with its usual tolerant lethargy.

'You'll only want your exercise books and pens today,' I said. I watched their faces curtain still more. A test, they thought.

'Look. There's a spider on the wall, a huge one. Quick—write down the first thing which comes into your head about it. Now—as quickly as you can.'

Startled eyes jumped to the wall, incredulous eyes looked back at me. What is she getting at? April fooling?

'Make it brief and snappy—don't stop to think just write what *you* feel,' I urged.

Hesitantly, at first, pens scratched on books, but before they had had time to cross out, correct or alter——

'Start on the next line, and say something about its body. Describe it as *you* see it.'

This time they started more easily, a bit strange, but still——

'Another new line and write three adjectives about its legs.'

'Now write of its web. Do you see any contrast between the spider and the web? Now round it off with a final sentence.'

As they were writing, I stood silently, feeling the revulsion against the spider, real and intense, and hoping that some miracle would happen to cause these children to have the same feeling and to be able to write it down without any words having been given to them.

This time I prayed before I opened the books. 'Please, just one. If only it has got through to just *one* of them.'

SPIDERS

Spiders are horrible and ugly, the very thought of
    them sends shivers down my spine.
This one has a bloated body, black and brown,
Its legs are long and spindly and fine,
The web is beautiful, dew-spangled, delicate,
But it is a trap.
The fly, though small, fights frantically, fiercely.

JANET STAINER

The first sentence showed me that the feeling had got through all right. The words, chosen quickly and emotionally were firm, descriptive and real.

I turned to the next one.

A nasty spider is clinging to the wall.
His body is bulgy, squashy, bloated.
His legs are hairy, horribly black.
The web is precise and elegant, tucked away in a
    corner,
To catch an ugly fly, it is a pity to use so beautiful
    a web.
When the fly is caught, it is wrapped and stored
    away
For ugly, hungry spider.

JENNIFER PRAGNELL

Here again, was the same grasp of words, as if the emotion itself supplied the right word almost without thought.

But these were girls, careful, anxious to please and to do the right thing. What of the boys?

Deliberately I searched through the pile and found the book of a slapdash, careless boy whose work was a constant battleground for him and for me.

> The spider is on the wall.
> Quickly I hit it with a newspaper.
> Its legs are long
> They look ghostly in the dark.
> Its body is fat, floppy and filthy,
> Its web looks like a net,
> A safety net in a circus.
> The web catches the flies
> The spider bites them,
> And wraps them,
> And keeps them,
> Until it is hungry.
>
> PHILIP SHEARS

This was more forthright than the girls' efforts, but here again was the same directness of expression and individuality of treatment which made these writings real and valuable.

Naturally I had the realist in the class who

started rather accusingly, 'I can't see a spider on the wall,' but he went on:

> I hate the things anyway.
> With bent skinny legs.
> Why do they have to be so swollen and stout?
> The beautiful web is a merciless trap for flies,
> They are a menace, a scrawny menace.

DAVID BEALE

So we were all satisfied.

Correction of the exercise, I found very simple. There were few spelling mistakes and, apart from an occasional grammatical slip, there was little to alter. One or two children, clinging to the conventional style, had found it difficult to break their work into lines, and needed to be shown how much more effective the writing *looked* if it was written out in this way, though, of course, if it was well read, the effect would be the same however it was written, so long as it was correctly punctuated. With regard to the 'breaking', I was most interested to find that so many children, right from the start, used a natural break with which to begin a new line, and that these breaks succeeded in giving the sentence its right, emotional value and balance. I will refer to this again.

Though it was obvious that the children wrote a form of modern verse, I never gave a hint that they were producing poetry, but now I started to encourage them to be aware of their use of words.

THE SPIDER'S WEDDING

I sat on the barn's steps and watched the black
spider coming towards me.

I felt like screaming

But I moved aside a little, and the dark creature
went up a beam.

It stopped

And turned back

And stared at me, and stared.

It said,

'Move on. My business has nothing to do with you.

I shall stand here until you go.'

So I moved on, looking back over my shoulder to see
what it would do.

As it went on, I ran back silently to see.

After a few minutes, back the spider came

Proud now, with an air of arrogance.

By his side, walked shyly, another spider.

A new bride.

When they came by me they stood

And stared and stared,

Then they went on.

'Ha. A spider's wedding,' I thought.

JUNE ROBINSON

We had lessons, for instance, on alliteration, which some children had used quite naturally and effectively in their first attempts. These lessons were quite apart from the creative writing periods, and, though I hoped that the result would be transferred, I didn't labour the point when the children were engaged in the written work.

Throughout the year, I had insisted that the children read as much and as widely as possible. I barred nothing except the out and out 'comic' and the modern, paper-backed travesty of a picture book. This, with the ever-present help of the television, had given the children a wide and good vocabulary, and I tried to encourage this by lessons on word associations and thought transference, showing how one word gives the thought of another. The children found this link most interesting to follow, with the natural result that their thoughts moved more freely and they discovered, to their surprise, that far from having not an idea in their heads as they had so often protested, having been given a start, ideas flowed in a most stimulating way and their thoughts quickened and became alive.

THE SPIDER

The spider is an ugly thing.
Its legs are long and hairy and jointed.
Its body is fat and ferocious,
It is not elegant at all.
I wonder that flies are attracted.
I would like to free the fly, but the spider might
    eat me.

CHRISTOPHER WATERS

The poem on page 15 was written some weeks later than the above, as a piece of free writing but it was obviously inspired by the early stimulus.

[3]

Being Alone

THE NEXT THING to do was to give this new expression a name. No word with a poetical or emotional bias would do, and it was while I was actually talking to the children about their work that the word *Intensive* came into my head. I hesitated to use it at first, for fear they should not fully understand the meaning, but no other word seemed to express what I wanted quite so well, and, as it happened, the children used it easily and correctly right from the start, so 'Intensive Writing' it became.

Now that the boat was launched, I was not so hesitant in my approach to *Intensive Writing*. I chose another fundamental fear—aloneness. With no preamble I asked the children to imagine that they were in a room by themselves, with darkness and a storm outside, and to write their thoughts. This time, it was no line by line effort, but they wrote the passage as a whole with as many or as few lines as they wished. I was interested to see that all the children settled down and wrote quickly without any pen biting or hesitation.

I felt that this was a sign that the stimulus, though in this case, terse and brief, had been quite adequate in giving them the right emotional push off, and also that I had chosen a subject which was well within the experience of all the children.

The results again delighted me by their directness, simplicity and rightness of word. I feel perhaps, that I must stress here that beyond telling the children to write what they felt, and to use words which came into their minds, I left the expression to come as a result of the emotion, rather than as a result of thought.

This is illustrated by the poems in this chapter.

IN THE DARK

I am by myself in a dark room.
The rain is beating on the roof, and the wind is
      howling.
The trees rustle in the dark.
A door creaks slowly.
A car rushes past.
Two owls hoot to each other and my ears grow
      big with listening.
I am frightened.

TEDDY WATERS

I am frightened.
Noises on the stairs,
Rain on the window,
The shadow of the curtain moving,
Moving.
The creak of the door,
The wind howling down the chimney
I am frightened.
I am frightened.

SUSAN BRIDGES

ALONE

The house was empty except for me,
Yet I was sure I wasn't alone.
What was that?
The wind, perhaps, in the trees.
A door creaked upstairs.
I shouted, 'Who's there?'
No one answered.
I waited, listening,
Holding my breath with fear.
I was alone and frightened.
Why didn't someone come?

CHRISTINE WILSON

On the whole, the boys did not produce writings with such honest emotions as the girls on this subject. Could it be that years of having to be unafraid had inhibited the boys and made it harder for them to express themselves freely? Or perhaps they are not so fearful about the dark. This is borne out by the result of one extra lesson which I had with the 14-year-olds. This same stimulus of being alone produced this gem from a boy.

GUILTY CONSCIENCE

I went to the shed for a cigarette. Mind, I was
    not allowed to smoke, and if Dad caught me,
    there's no telling *what* would happen.

I lit it

And puffed.

What's that?

Quick as a flash the cigarette is out and I stand
    with beating heart, waiting.

It was only the door, swinging and creaking in the
    evening breeze.

I lit up again

And puffed.

The door opened with a push and a clatter, hitting,
    storming, searching out the sinner.

Without waiting to think, I dashed out, down the
    path round the corner, and indoors.

Safe?

Safe from myself?

RODNEY SIVYOUR

This was the result of half an hour's teaching
on intensive writing.

The wind, blowing through the bare trees
Sounded like a ghost on that dark night.
Everything was still.
Quiet.
Except the wind,
And an owl hooting.
It was frightening.
I was so scared
In that haunted house
Alone on that dark night.

MARGARET CULLING

[24]

[4]

Fear

THESE TWO SUBJECTS, Spiders and Aloneness which I had given for intensive writing, flung the door wide open for a most interesting discussion with the children on Fear.

Children of twelve and thirteen, nowadays, are very much aware of world events. I suppose that Television, Wireless, and Newspapers blare with such headlines that none of us can escape, and the fact that children don't really understand scientific and political trends, does nothing to alleviate the anxiety which they feel.

From their talk in the discussion on the causes of fear, and its results, it was obvious that these children live with a fatalistic acceptance of war as an inevitable result of scientific research.

'When do you think the war will start?' they

asked me, and 'Who do you think we shall fight against?' 'How many miles will the Bomb blow up?' This negative acceptance of the Slough of Despondency seemed to me to be the wrong attitude. With childlike eyes of wisdom they could see the futility but they felt powerless to do anything but accept the situation.

> The trouble in the world today is caused by fear.
> One country fears another
> Because of atom bombs
> Or outer space missiles.
> Its daft I think.
> They spend money on weapons
> And have no money left
> To clothe and feed the people.

> DIANE STRUTT

As intensive writing, this did not please so much. It lacked the vigour which I had noted before, and, strangely enough, all the writing seemed enfeebled by the children's hopeless negative attitude.

FEAR

Think of all the people who are afraid.

Black people fear white people,

White people fear yellow people

Americans fear Russians,

Indians fear Chinese,

English fear Germans,

And so on.

A never ending stream of fear which is flooding the
world.

It has made hatred,

It has made cruelty,

It has made the Atom Bomb.

What can we do to stop being afraid?

This was a class effort with the children con-
tributing freely but still we didn't feel satisfied. It
was left to one boy to provide the perfect solution.
A quiet, thoughtful boy, whose written English
had been, up to now, careful but uninspired.
He wrote quietly for a time.

FEAR CONQUERED?

Years before He was born
People thought He would come to save them.
When He was born
Kings came to worship Him.
He grew up in poverty
And was betrayed
For thirty pieces of silver.
He died.
And three days later, rose again.
His life was an example of how love conquers fear.
But the scientists of today
Make bombs,
Lots of bombs
To blow each other up, and prove themselves
The better men.

JOHN WHITE

This was intensive writing at its very best;
complete simplicity of language, clarity of thought,
and a positive, individual approach.

[5]

Spring Ting-a-Ling

FEAR HAD BEEN sticky, with a triumphant climax, but the next effort was a complete failure. The weather had been perfect, with that breathtaking perfection of new life. Spring has been an inspiration for generations. Here, at last, I felt on safe ground. One sight of the bursting buds, one sniff of the balmy air, and they would be off with the most inspired writing I had had up to date. And, of course, the day of the lesson dawned wet and cold. Now, I know that the writing should have been postponed, but then, I thought that the inspiration could be recalled from the previous day. I gave a short pep talk, recalling blue skies, and warm sunshine, and left them to it. Cold, grey skies lowered dismally, the wind howled around the bleak playground, rain spattered against the dirty panes.

'Spring is here again
How pretty are the little birds
Which fly up in the sky'

or

'Spring is here as you will know
All the flowers around you see
The trees send out their blossoms sweet
To brighten the sky.'

It was obviously the honesty which was lacking, and it taught me a valuable lesson. Intensive writing cannot be falsified or sentimentalised. It will only come out right if the feeling with which it is written is real, alive, and vital to the writer. Nor can it be produced by second-hand experiences. To observe, to think, to feel for oneself is essential.

Surely in this world of brainwashings, clichés, platitudes and lies, it is important that education should strive to encourage this honest self-expression ?

The very next fine day, I took all the children out into the Recreation Ground, which is a large open field just opposite the school. I asked the children to scatter, and for ten minutes just to absorb all the freshness and activity that went on around them. Some lay down on the grass, some strolled quietly about, but all used their eyes and ears and hearts. What a difference when they came to express what they had really seen and felt.

WRITTEN IN MAY

The sky, blue, dotted with feathery white clouds,
    gives a bright roof to the world.
The swifts, swerving and twirling, twist in the
    bright roof.
Far below them lies a carpet of green, dotted with
    white and yellow.
The bees buzz in the clover heads,
A pheasant calls distantly across the fields,
Among the crisp new leaves the small birds twitter,
Oh! Isn't May wonderful?

DIANE FLETCHER

OPEN AIR LESSON

The sky is clear, new-washed and clean.

The fresh grass is spread like a velvet carpet.

All around, the trees stand like sentinels,

Or perhaps, like models now, for they are beautiful
    with blossom.

The hawthorn is white,

The shining copper beech stands darkly in the
    corner,

The chestnuts hold up their spikes of pink and
    white,

All the trees cast dark shadows on us.

It is very beautiful here today.

JANE BEASLEY

[*6*]

Snake

MY OWN INTEREST in modern verse had been re-aroused by the children's work and I started to read again, with pleasure, the poems of T. S. Eliot, Dylan Thomas and D. H. Lawrence. It was from this last writer that I took my next stimulus for the children. 'Snake', though set in Sicilian scenery, was perfectly comprehensible to country children who had had their own experiences of killing adders.

I read the poem through, explaining nothing, hoping that the rightness of the words would be enough. The children listened intently, no masked faces now, for this was intensive writing to them, not that cissy, poetry stuff. I said to them, 'You have all had some experience with a bird or animal or insect. You have stood and looked as that man did at the snake. Write down what you saw and thought.'

Without hesitation, up came their pens and they started. This was a winner. All children are fascinated by animal life. Country children have the opportunity to indulge in this fascination freely, and the ideas and thoughts tumbled on to the paper. They reminisced eagerly as I looked at their work.

'*That* was the time I fell in the river. My mother was awfully cross', and 'It made me dreadfully late watching, but it was jolly good'.

The enthusiasm had bubbled through into the writing. This poem is by Raymond Thackeray.

KINGFISHER

I lay still, watching, listening,
I wanted to fidget but I daren't,
So I lay still on the feathery grass by the water's
    edge
And watched.
There he was, blue coated, elegant, graceful.

He dived and curved and swooped and circled
Like a blue flame.
I was fascinated, fidgets forgotten.
Then suddenly,
He dropped like a stone down, down,
Down into the water.
Then up and a gleam of silver as the fish was
   swallowed.
I thought,
'How could this bird
Beautiful and elegant
Be so cruel?'
I said to myself,
'Not cruel, but Nature.'

SLOW-WORM

I saw a slow-worm in the grass.

I went to catch it,

When suddenly I said,

'I'll watch and see what it does.'

It slithered slippily through the grass.

A fly!

It stopped

And slid round to the back of the fly

Silently,

Slowly.

As quick as lightning its tongue shot out and caught
the fly

And I dived and caught it.

I would keep it as a pet,

I would take it to school.

It was mine.

But Dad said, 'Let it go, son.'

So I did.

And it slid happily into the sunshine

Free again.

TEDDY WATERS

[36]

THE HARES

Two hares came lolloping over the field.

Suddenly they sat up.

I crouched low, watching.

Then they began to box,

Hitting at each other with their paws,

Ducking and dodging,

I stopped breathing for fear they would see me.

Closer they came.

Five yards, four yards,

Dodging and ducking,

Swaying backwards and forwards

To and fro.

They stopped suddenly,

Gazing towards me

And darted off, weaving in and out of the hedge all

    the way up to the field and into the woods.

Slowly I got up and went off.

EDDIE SMITH

These two poems illustrate well the way the
children used the break of the line to stress the

feeling, of which I have spoken in a previous chapter. The short lines

> 'Silently
>
> Slowly.'

give the pause followed by the scurry of 'As quick as lightning its tongue shot out and caught the fly.'

You can watch the two hares dart off 'weaving in and out of the hedge all the way up to the field and into the woods'. It is satisfying and right because the number of words used are fitted to the feeling.

THE FLIES

Two great, blue flies buzzed around the window.
Their bodies shone.
Their wings made a humming sound on the pane.
Then the cloud of fly spray hit them.
The spraying liquid hit the flies.
Twisting and writhing in all directions, they fell
    on their backs.
Their long, spiny legs kicked.
Their long, lean, spiny legs kicked in a death dance.
Furiously buzzing on their backs, they were
    helpless.
They grew weaker.
Their legs were tired.
Their bodies were slow.
Gradually they stopped,
One after another.
It was still and very quiet.

ALAN KING

Somehow I feel that Wordsworth would have approved of this simple everyday subject for poetry.

The girls were much more domesticated than the boys in their choice of subjects. Their pets hold first place in their hearts, and it was mice and horses, dogs and cats which inspired them.

THE MOUSE

A tiny black-velvet coated mouse crept along the floor.

He went slowly at first, then quickened his pace.

When he reached his dish, he picked several pieces of brown corn in his black paws and nibbled away.

All the time his shiny, black eyes were glancing about the cage.

Then he sat up and washed himself.

His short, rough, pink tongue popped quickly out of his mouth and in again.

After making sure his fat, little body was clean he inspected himself from top to toe.

Then he laid himself down in a nest of golden straw and went to sleep.

All this time I had been peering round the side of the cage, watching him.

JANET READ

THE MICE

Early one morning, when I went to see the mouse, I found that she had six babies. I watched her making a nest to keep them warm. She scurried about, finding pieces of straw. Then she lay down with them, so they could snuggle against her, finding warmth and food. I put some corn in the cage. Out she came and nibbled until she was full, then back she went to the babies. This she would do all day long keeping watch over them.

SANDRA NOYCE

THE CAT

Sleekly smooth and shimmering,
Eyes alive,
Ears alert,
The cat, moving only to twitch her tail,
Her tail, long, thin, hair bristling at the tip,
The bird flies, and she mews and jumps down from
    her perch on the window sill,
Light footed, she stalks to the door
And waits, silently, patiently.

DIANE STRUTT

D

[41]

One girl, who would dearly love a horse of her own, did some wishful thinking and produced this imaginative piece.

THE FOAL

I lay on the grass whispering silly little words to my mare who was steadily eating grass. I was asleep.

I was in Africa. My mare was going to have a foal. She lay on the grass. She would not get up. I went quickly and ran and fetched a man and soon the foal was there. It was beautiful and I was happy. But suddenly, there was a slimy thing. A snake. It slithered to the foal. I got a stick. I fought but the snake was strong. He bit once and the foal screamed. I took his lifeless head and laid it on the soft grass. I wept.

I awoke and blinked. The sun was warm on my face. I was glad it was a dream.

JANET TAYLOR

I have a suspicion that psychiatrists would read something into that one, but, wish fulfilment or not, I felt it was sensitive and honest.

The close and careful observation of animals and birds is shown well in the next two pieces.

THE TORTOISE

A slow dirty tortoise moved clumsily across the cage,
His rough skin rasped under the heavy shell.
His eyes stared like small black pebbles, hard, unwinkingly.
As he reached the soft green lettuce leaf, his mouth split.
Toothlessly he munched, the leaf gradually disappearing.

WENDY CULLING

THE THRUSH

A thrush on the lawn kept looking with his small round eye. Then he would make a dive to see if a worm was there. When he had eaten, he flew away but came back quickly, landing gracefully with a little curtsy. He stood listening. He hopped once, twice, three times. . . . Then listened again. He repeated this several times before he got his worm.

JENNIFER STREET

They obviously have a vivid picture in their own minds, which they are able to reproduce clearly, because they are concentrating upon the pictures and not worrying about what words to use.

The nearest subject to wild life which came from the girls was a very forceful effort. The following episode, she told me, she actually saw, and a very frightening experience it must have been for Margaret Culling.

THE FIGHT

We stopped to have lunch among the trees of the
New Forest.

A mare was standing a little way away, watching
two stallions.

They were fighting, probably over **her.**

One was jet black

The other was a skewbald, with an evil look in his
eye.

I wanted to look away, but I couldn't.

I wanted to throw something at them, but I
couldn't.

All I could do was to watch, fascinated, terrified.

They fought fiercely, kicking, biting, squealing.

Then the black stallion fell to his knees.

Instantly, like lightning, the skewbald lashed out
and kicked him on the head.

The skewbald stood still.

The black stallion lay flat.

He was still.

He didn't move at all.

He was dead.

MARGARET CULLING

This set of intensive writing on animals assured me that I was on the right track. I felt now that I had succeeded in giving the children a medium of expression which they could use easily and happily and which produced results which satisfied me. It was quite exciting.

The Weaker Brethren

BUT WAS IT exciting for everybody? What impact was this new kind of expression having upon the children who always find school work difficult or even impossible. I'm sure that every rural school has them in every class and even the big town schools, though in the latter, the children can be streamed, and special teaching given to the slower ones. We have in our school, children who have been recommended to Special Schools, but as there is no room for them, they must remain with us. What of them?

My policy has always been, as far as is humanly possible, to let these children feel that they are normal,—slower, perhaps, requiring more help, but that they can finally achieve a result which is comparable to that reached by the other children.

For instance, I would never teach a senior child to read by using an infant book. Senior children need senior tools and a senior outlook, though it must be geared to the individual requirement of the child. I feel that this method succeeds by the fact that in my classes every child will 'have a go' at everything. No blank books are sent in and no one says, 'I can't do that'. So when we started intensive writing everyone joined in, and because I was only asking for the children's own thoughts, expressed simply and briefly, even those whose thoughts were not so profound, whose expression was not so polished, found no handicap in putting down their own simple sentences, and they had the satisfaction of knowing that they had achieved what was asked of them.

> A spider crauls up the wall
> The spider is ugly
> His web is strong
> The fly stuk himself in the web.

This—with the original spelling—is the work of a boy who is officially E.S.N. I have deliberately left the spelling mistakes in and reproduced this as it was written in order to show that when children write with an emotion as a driving force, spelling and grammar seem to come right more easily. Ask the psychologists why this should be so. All I can say is, that when any work is done with personal interest, it usually flows along smoothly and easily, because the concentration of thought is on the finished creation, not on how it is being done.

THE OLD HOUSE

It was very cold and raining hard.
A big white owl was sweeping around.
The wind blew in.
A mouse ran into the straw, rustling.
A horse whinnied out in the field.
I started to cry.
I was frightened in the dark.
It was silent in the dark.

This is the work of a boy who finds all school lessons very difficult. He is tough and alive and likeable and talks with great enthusiasm of his experiences. I am hoping that intensive writing will give him a chance to be able to express himself in writing as well as he does orally.

WRITTEN IN MAY

The sun is shining bright,
The dew is still on the ground
There is a white drift of may on the hedge.
The birds are singing, and the swifts are playing
high above my head.
The daisies and buttercups are scattered here and
there, looking very gay.

This boy is almost certainly a 'late developer' (what horrible phrases we use in the educational world). His work has been babyish, as though he were afraid to tackle the complications of senior thoughts and expressions, but now that he is encouraged to write simply, there are signs of more mature thought—'a white drift of may in the hedge', or 'the swifts are playing high above my head', which are pleasing and satisfying both to the boy and to me.

I think it is the feeling that I believe that their thoughts are important enough to write down, which gives these children confidence.

One girl, thinking of miracles, wrote:

> The way a cat's fur grows
> And stays,
> The way our hair grows
> And has to be cut and cut,
> Surely that's a miracle.

And a few lines later:

> The way a watch ticks when it is wound.
> The way we talk
> And walk
> And run.

You can understand the amazement as the girl suddenly realised the miracle of growth and movement, both natural and mechanical, and the pride that she has thought of it.

Understanding—is it this, to which these children are responding? I'm sure that all of us feel more confident in ourselves when we know that we are not isolated or peculiar in our thoughts and ideas; that we have a kinship with the rest of humanity; that other people think as we do, and can understand and approve so that we no longer feel that we have to hide our ideas and pretend we don't think at all, for fear people will dub us odd or silly.

I am certain that intensive writing has given, not only to retarded children, but also to children who are emotionally shy and lacking in confidence, the opportunity to express themselves, and so find themselves. Strangely enough, some of the most successful writings have been done by children who, up to now, have been in the lower half of the class. The introspective children, the shut-in children, the children who 'could do better', are

given, at last, the opportunity to write willingly and eagerly, their own private thoughts and fears and hopes, and we have stood amazed at the beauty of the results.

IN THE MORNING

An old oak tree,
Early in the morning with the golden dewdrops on
    the crisp green grass,
A young squirrel
In earnest to see its new life, scrambles down the
    rotten bark
To where a robin drinks hurriedly by the pool.

The writer of that is awkward, a problem child, a boy who has had no success. For obvious reasons, I have used no names in this chapter, but to me these are the children whose names should be shouted to the sky, for these are the successes of intensive writing, those who couldn't, but now who can; those for whom the door has opened, letting them pass triumphantly through to join their hitherto more successful companions.

[8]

Miracles

As soon as I found Walt Whitman's 'Miracles', I knew that it would be ideal as a stimulus for a set of intensive writing. The children were intrigued when I read it, and, I was amazed to find, inclined to be critical.

'Are all those "ors" good?' they asked. 'Surely it is wrong to keep using the same word?'

It gave me a good chance to talk of the power of repetition—and at the same time I had a private ponder over how much harm we do to children's expression when we make these rigid, set rules, such as 'Never start a sentence with "and"', 'Don't use the same word twice', 'Be careful not to end with a preposition', and so on. Confronted by these hurdles and obstacles, the children can lose the race even before they start.

Art suffered in a similar way, until the children wisely threw off the shackles of perspective and convention, and painted as *they* saw and felt; with stimulating results.

Writing, I feel, must do likewise.

But back to miracles.

The poem certainly stimulated a great deal of thought among the children. Until then, miracles had had a Biblical connection only, to them. Although they no doubt had talked loosely of some unexpected joyful happening as being 'miraculous', they had never thought that the intense wonder which they had in the world around them was due to miracles.

Now they started to look with new eyes.

MIRACLES

The tiny chick
Grows in the egg, and knows by a miracle
When it should peck
And peck
And force a way out of its prison.

JENNIFER STREET

Air, fresh, unbelievably soft.
The sea rippling on the shore,
Waves with white foam,
The cruel rocks
And children's voices filled with laughter as they
  play on the sand.
Miracles, we must believe.

SALLY ANNETTS

The children grappled with their own thoughts
and put them down clearly.

I sometimes think about the sun
And wonder why it doesn't go away
And leave us in the dark.

JOHN WHITE

The whole world is full of miracles, though people
  don't seem to realise it.
The sea which thunders against the rocks,
Leaves which whisper in the wind,
Flowers which light the world with colour,
Darkness and Light,
What miracles there are in the world!

VICTORIA GILBERT

Birds flying
Gave men an idea to make something with wings
Which miraculously could fly, too—
An aeroplane.

JOHN WHITE

Where the thought would not come clearly, the child was not afraid to say so.

A miracle?
What is it?
I don't know for sure.
The birds, the flowers, the trees,
They're all miracles.
We are miracles
With our talking, hearing, seeing,
With our walking, running, dancing,
Yes, we *are* miracles.

DIANE STRUTT

As the thoughts, though unsure, are expressed, so you feel the child is getting through to a solution which is acceptable because it satisfies her. 'Yes we *are* miracles.'

I felt very pleased by this spate of individual thought, for while the stimulus had been given by Walt Whitman, the children had obviously, not merely trodden meekly where his thoughts had gone, but had frisked off to pastures of their own. They were at last gaining confidence in their own ideas, and putting them forward even to stand against a great writer and thinker.

The second thing that pleased me when I read this set of intensive writing was that the children were becoming more and more aware of the value of words. They were discovering that they could clothe thoughts in beauty by choosing the correct words.

Whether *The Moon* is a derivative from the Walt Whitman line, 'Or the exquisite, delicate, thin curve of the new moon in Spring', or not, the writer has taken it to herself, and from her own thoughts has created a passage of beauty.

So is this long-delayed tribute to Spring, which came now with a different, more honest stimulus.

THE MOON

Then comes the lovely, soothing ghostly moon
Walking with silvery feet across the sky,
Not like the hot, bright, bustling sun,
But calm, serene.
As the days change
The moon changes too,
A round ball,
A half ball,
A thin strip
Then nothing at all.
This indeed is a great miracle.

HELEN SIM

SPRING

So soft, so silent, so slender
Snowdrops with white bells,
The lovely tangy smell of primroses,
Birds busy in the woods,
The drift of green over the copse.
The miracle of Spring.

CAROL BUDDEN

It is appropriate to end a chapter on miracles with a miracle. The following passage was written by a boy whose normal essays invariably ended 'Then we watched Telly, then we went to bed'.

MIRACLES

I was walking through a big, high wood,
I was tired and very hot,
So I sat down by a great, old oak tree.
'What is a miracle?' I asked myself.
'Is it a seed that is put into the ground
And shoots up in bloom like a flower?
Or is it the sun shining on the leaves?'
All of a sudden, rain beats against the old tree,
The bark feels like hard, rough tin.
The rain tries to fight its way through the hard
    baked ground
Which suddenly opens its mouth and drinks eagerly
So the seed will grow.
Is it a miracle?

MAURICE YEATES

It certainly was to me.

Let the Children Write

THERE WAS NO doubt that in three months, the children had taken intensive writing to their hearts, and were beginning to feel the value of it for themselves. Still, they did not realise that they were sometimes writing poetry; they wrote in the way that best expressed how they felt. Nor did they realise that they were doing anything different from other children. Two girls who had had an interview for second-chance scholarships, came back most indignant because the interviewer knew nothing of intensive writing. 'She said that she had never heard of it,' they said, in astonishment.

I learned just how much it meant to them, after a night of violent and prolonged thunderstorms which had swept the area for hours, keeping us all awake and frightened. Among the tired and wan faces in the Assembly Hall, the next morning, my class glowed.

'Frightened? Of course I wasn't. I was thinking all the time about what I should put in my intensive writing.'

So it had developed that I need not longer stimulate the emotion—that the children could look at life and life itself would give the stimulus to make them want to write.

THE STORM

The howl of the wind in the wires,
The pattering rain on window and roof.
The rustlings in the hedges,
The creakings of the fences,
Suddenly the lightning flashes,
The thunder explodes
And rumbles across the black sky.
But soon all will be still and quiet
As the night creeps on to bring another day.

IAN HILLS

[64]

In their spare time, I would see children busily writing, as some idea came into their heads which they felt they could express. They were writing now, not because they had to, but because they wanted to. This poem is by Malcolm Hills:

VENOM

The long litheness of a snake's slippery sundrenched
    skin
Sliding through the grass, silently,
One fatal move—
And sharp fangs pierce.
Pain!
All you know is pain!
Writhing pain!
Death.

THE OLD MAN

Watching at the door,
Listening to the blackbird,
Stands the old man.
Not wanting to go in
But dreaming of past happiness,
Of warm and sunny days,
Of laughter and dance,
When his feet were nimble and his wit was quick,
Then the chattering children
Running on their way from school
Waken him, and he shuffles in
And shuts the door on his dreams.

CAROL PENN-MULLENS

I wonder if I have given the impression that
we had, by now abandoned the conventional
type of essay writing. Of course, nothing is farther
from the truth. Many of the children of this age
group sat for an external examination in June, and
I had to make sure that they could tackle the
papers which were set. Every week, as usual, the
children wrote a three-page essay, and I marked

it. It was not until the end of the term that I found the idea had percolated through from intensive writing to essay writing. This is the beginning of an examination essay by Alan King.

Three, two, one, zero. A thundering noise clapped the side of the mountains. The rocket rose skyward, its destination the Moon. The first man, on his way to the moon, was off! Throughout the world scientists and astronomers watched as he rose steadily into the heavens. He was in another world, a vast world, a frightening world. He was alone. Any perils he must fight himself.

As he swung up towards the moon, he noticed, against the dark sky, a group of small, coloured, lights, rushing towards him.

'Meteorites?', he asked himself.

For anyone who is interested, the coloured lights turned out to be Space Ships from another planet, which involved the pilot in many hair-raising adventures. But that does not detract from the pleasure I felt when I read the first, well-written page.

[*10*]

'And the World says'

I HAD TOLD the children many times, that I was sure they had it in them to write just as well as many authors whose work was published, and, to encourage them, we produced a booklet in June called INTENSIVE WRITING.

We are a poor school, and to find enough school paper on which to duplicate the work was impossible. I managed to get a ream of paper although it meant that I **had the** heartbreaking task of choosing a limited number of writings, so that we didn't use too much. The cover was even more of a headache, and we were just on the point of launching our new production in a naked state when I had the unexpected gift of a bundle of old X-ray film covers. (They are usually burned as waste.) Their cheerful orange colour gave the outside of our booklet, a lovely, gay, devil-may-care appearance.

The booklet met with a very mixed reception in school. The authors, whose work had been selected, were jubilant; the authors whose work had been rejected, solely for lack of paper, were huffy; the Staff were non-committal.

By now, I felt that I must know for sure, whether I was deluding myself or not.

I chose the most authoritative educational paper I knew, packed up our unpretentious pamphlet, X-ray cover and all, and sent it off, with a covering note asking what the editor felt about it.

Things started to happen with a vengeance. The paper published an article which brought us letters from all over the country. And not only letters.

It culminated in a phone call, asking if an American press representative could visit us. As it was the last day of the Summer term, with all its turning out, packing in, and breaking up, I'm afraid our welcome to him, though warm, was breathless.

Fortunately, the children took him to their hearts. They waited patiently while he admired the thatched roof and thick ancient walls. They combed their hair and posed perfectly with dry pens (no ink, of course), hovering over full books (no paper left), while he took innumerable photographs of them supposedly doing their 'Intensive Writing'. He asked if he could speak to the children in twos or threes, and immediately they formed themselves into excited groups.

In between my columns of register results, lists of books, and piles of reports, I caught a glimpse of him at the Staff Room door, surrounded by eager, enthusiastic children, offering to be the next for interview. I could hear their voices, alive, full of interest and individuality.

And as they talked now, so they wrote.

[*11*]

Several Months Later

THE CHILDREN at Winterslow are working on an anthology of 'Intensive Writing', which grows week by week. To this collection we hope to add contributions of other writers from all over the world. Young apprentices in Industry, Kikiyu girls in Africa, Israeli children, American teen-agers, all are trying out this system and finding that it works. People from Canada, Germany, Australia, Holland, Malaya have written with interest and enthusiasm. I feel that if only inter-national affairs were conducted with the honesty and simplicity which 'Intensive Writing' de-mands, there would be a great deal more hope for the world. Naturally, the children's horizons have been widened beyond the confines of Winterslow. Their imaginations, set free at last, move far over the world and beyond.

In the velvet blue blackness
Millions of stars appear,
Moving in set order with their trailing moons.
We are more minute than a microscopic creature
      against the vastness of this galaxy.
Man's future mind
Makes vehicles to conquer the immensity of Space.
For what?
Man's home is here.

JOHN MILLS